Gone Forever!

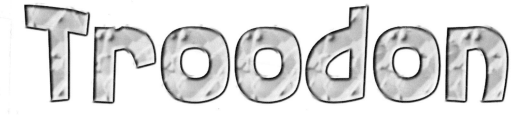

Troodon

Rupert Matthews

Heinemann Library
Chicago, Illinois

Customer Service 888-454-2279
Visit our website at www.heinemannlibrary.com

Produced for Heinemann Library by White-Thomson Publishing Ltd.
Edited by Kay Barnham
Book design by John Jamieson
Concept design by Ron Kamen and Paul Davies & Associates
Illustrations by James Field (SGA)
Originated by Que-Net Media™
Printed and bound in China by South China Printing Company

08 07 06 05 04
10 9 8 7 6 5 4 3 2 1

Library of Congress Cataloging-in-Publication Data
Matthews, Rupert.
  Troodon / Rupert Matthews.
      p. cm. -- (Gone forever!)
Summary: Discusses the dinosaur Troodon, including its known physical characteristics, behavior, habitat, and what other creatures were contemporaneous with it, as well as how scientists study fossils and evaluate geological features to learn about extinct organisms.
Includes bibliographical references and index.
  ISBN 1-4034-4914-7 (hardcover) -- ISBN 1-4034-4921-X (pbk.)
  1. Troodon--Juvenile literature. [1. Troodon. 2. Dinosaurs.] I.
Title.
  QE862.S3M33255 2004
  567.912--dc22

                                    2003016686

Acknowledgments
The author and publisher are grateful to the following for permission to reproduce copyright material:
Cover photograph reproduced with permission of Museum of the Rockies, Montana.
p. 4 Peter Menzel/Science Photo Library; pp. 6, 8, 20, 26 Royal Tyrell Museum/Alberta Community Development; pp. 10, 16, 18, 22, 24 American Museum of Natural History; p. 12 Museum of the Rockies, Montana; p. 14 GeoScience.

Special thanks to Dr. Peter Makovicky of the Chicago Field Museum for his review of this book.

shown in bold, **like this.** You can
ey mean by looking in the glossary.

Contents

Gone Forever!

Some animals are **extinct.**
This means that there
are none left alive anywhere in the
world. Scientists called **paleontologists** learn
about extinct animals by studying their **fossils.**

Troodon was a type of **dinosaur** that lived
in North America millions of years ago.
Paleontologists have found fossils of Troodon.
They study these fossils to discover what
Troodon looked like when it was alive.

Troodon's Home

Troodon **fossils** have been found in rocks in North America. Scientists called **geologists** study these rocks. They learn what the place was like when Troodon lived there.

Troodon lived in a land that was warm. Some months of the year were very rainy. Troodon may have lived on low hills, near larger mountains. Between the hills there were wide valleys.

7

Plants and Trees

Paleontologists have found plant **fossils** in the same rocks as the fossils of Troodon. The fossils show what plants grew at the time of Troodon.

plant
fossil

Most plants were like modern bushes, such as roses, **magnolias,** and **brambles.** Troodon may have lived among thick bushes and **shrubs.** A few trees grew among the bushes.

Living with Troodon

Other **dinosaurs** lived at the time of Troodon. Some dinosaurs, such as **Chasmosaurus** and **Albertosaurus,** were much larger than Troodon.

Chasmosaurus skull

Large **herds** of Chasmosaurus moved through the valleys. They ate the leaves and twigs of bushes and trees. Albertosaurus was a huge hunter that liked to eat Chasmosaurus.

Albertosaurus

Chasmosaurus

Troodon

What Was Troodon?

Paleontologists study the **fossils** of Troodon to find out what sort of animal it was. The teeth show what kind of food it ate. The leg bones show how quickly it could run. Marks on the bones show where the **muscles** grew.

Troodon skeleton

Troodon was a meat-eating **dinosaur** that
fed on small animals. It could run very quickly.
It used its claws to catch **prey.**

Troodon Eggs

Paleontologists have found the **fossils** of Troodon nests. They have studied the nests to find out how an adult Troodon protected its eggs from egg-eating animals.

egg fossils

Troodon kept its nest very safe. It built a small mound, laid its eggs inside, then sat on top to keep them warm. Troodon would attack any other animal that came too close to the nest.

Growing Up

After several days, the young Troodons hatched out of the eggs. **Fossils** of young **dinosaurs** have not been found near the nests. This means that the young Troodons left the nest almost at once.

insect fossil

The adult dinosaurs probably showed their young how to find other animals. Then the young Troodons may have caught their own food. At first the young probably hunted small animals, such as beetles or insects. They may have eaten worms.

The Hunting Pack

Paleontologists have studied the skull of Troodon. They have found that the **dinosaur** had a very large **brain** compared to the size of its body. This shows that Troodon was one of the smartest dinosaurs.

brain fossil

Troodon may have used its brain to hunt.
A single Troodon would not have been able
to attack a larger animal. Instead, several
Troodons may have hunted as a **pack.**

Top Speed

Troodon's front legs were short with long claws. They were used to grab food. The **dinosaur's** back legs were long and powerful. They had wide feet and short, wide claws.

Troodon leg fossil

The claws on Troodon's back feet gripped the ground as it ran. Troodon could change direction very quickly by digging its claws into the ground.

Special Eyes

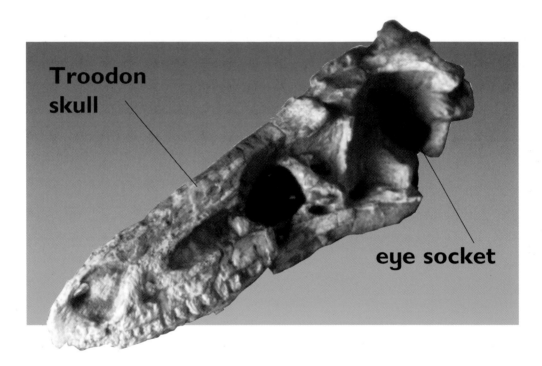

Troodon skull

eye socket

Troodon had large eyes, which helped it see well in poor light. The **dinosaur** may have hunted at **dusk,** or by moonlight, when other dinosaurs were asleep.

Most dinosaurs had eyes on the sides of their heads. **Fossils** show that Troodon's eyes were closer to the front of its head. The eyes could look forward, so it could see better than other dinosaurs.

What Did Troodon Eat?

hadrosaur skull

Scientists have found other animal **fossils** near the fossils of Troodon. There are fossils of several types of **dinosaurs** called **hadrosaurs.** Troodon may have fed on these creatures.

The hadrosaurs had no natural weapons with which to defend themselves. A **pack** of Troodons would have been strong enough to attack the larger dinosaur. One hadrosaur would have fed a whole pack of Troodons.

A Quick Snack

Didelphodon jaw fossil

The **fossils** of small **mammals** have also been found near Troodon fossils. Mammals are animals with fur or hair. Most large animals alive today are mammals, including humans.

Didelphodon was a mammal that lived at about the same time and in the same place as Troodon. A lone Troodon might have hunted and eaten small animals like Didelphdon. It may also have eaten **lizards,** birds, and other small animals.

Where Did Troodon Live?

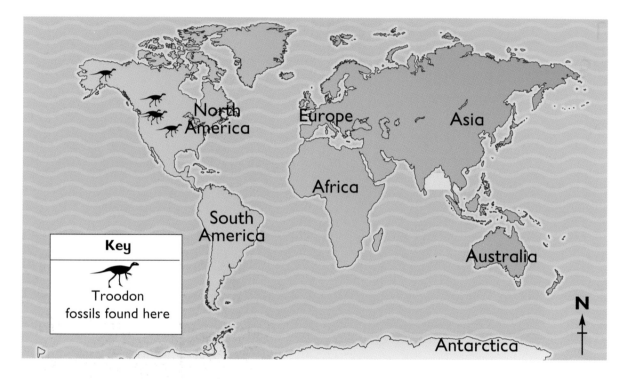

Key

Troodon fossils found here

North America

Europe

Asia

Africa

South America

Australia

Antarctica

N

Troodon **fossils** have been found in parts of North America. Troodon lived in places that are now part of Montana, Wyoming, and Alaska in the United States, and Alberta in Canada.

When Did Troodon Live?

Troodon lived between 76 and 70 million years ago. It lived near the end of the Cretaceous period, which was part of the Mesozoic era. The Mesozoic era is also known as the Age of the Dinosaurs.

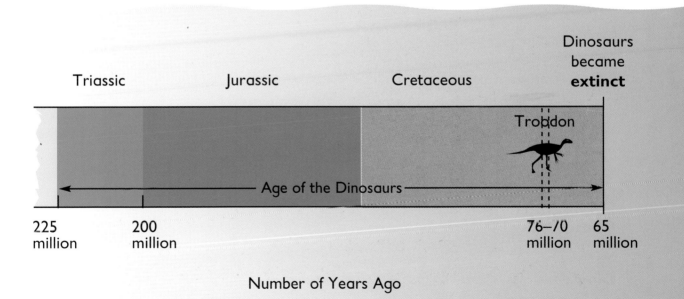

Triassic   Jurassic   Cretaceous   Dinosaurs became **extinct**

Troodon

←————————— Age of the Dinosaurs —————————→

225 million   200 million   76–70 million   65 million

Number of Years Ago

Fact File

Troodon	
Length:	up to 8 feet (2.5 meters)
Height:	up to 3 feet (1 meter)
Weight:	up to 110 pounds (50 kg)
Time:	late Cretaceous period, about 75 million years ago
Place:	North America

How to Say It

Albertosaurus—al-ber-toe-sawr-us

Chasmosaurus—kaz-mo-sawr-us

Cretaceous—kreh-tay-shus

Didelphodon—dy-delf-o-don

dinosaur—dine-o-sawr

hadrosaur—had-ro-sawr

Jurassic—jer-as-ik

Mesozoic—meh-so-zo-ik

paleontologist—pay-lee-on-tah-lo-jist

prey—pray

Triassic—try-as-ik

Troodon—tro-o-don

Glossary

Albertosaurus meat-eating dinosaur that hunted other dinosaurs

brain organ of thought located inside the skull that is also the control point for the nervous system

bramble prickly plant

Chasmosaurus plant-eating dinosaur with three horns and a large frill

Didelphodon extinct mammal that had a pouch and was the size of a dog

dinosaur reptile that lived on Earth between 228 and 65 million years ago but has died out

dusk time of day when the sun is setting and it is getting dark

extinct once lived on Earth but has died out

fossil remains of a plant or animal, usually found in rocks

geologist scie   rocks

hadrosaur plant-eating dinosaur

herd group of animals that live together

lizard small reptile with a long tail

magnolia tree or bush, usually with creamy-white flowers

mammal warm-blooded animal with a backbone and hair or fur. Mammals give birth to live young that feed on milk from the mother's body.

muscle part of an animal's body that makes it move

pack group of hunting animals

paleontologist scientist who studies the fossils of animals or plants that have died out

prey animal that is hunted and eaten by other animals

shrub woody plant that has several stems and is smaller than rees

More Books to Read

Anthony, Laurence. *Looking at Troodon (Cretaceous Period)*. Milwaukee, Wis.: Gareth Stevens, 1997.

Davis, Kenneth C. *Don't Know Much about Dinosaurs*. New York: Harper Collins, 2004.

Scott, Janine. *Discovering Dinosaurs*. Minneapolis, Minn.: Compass Point, 2002.

Index